# Fun With Friends

Sheryl Silverman

Photographs by
Fernando and Barbara Batista

**HAMPTON-BROWN BOOKS**
MANY CULTURES, MANY LANGUAGES…MANY POSSIBILITIES!™

Fun for two.

Fun for three.

Fun for four.

Fun for five.

Fun for six.

Fun for everyone!